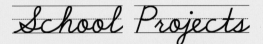

School Projects
SURVIVAL
GUIDES

Oral Reports

Barbara A. Somervill

Heinemann Library
Chicago, Illinois

© 2009 Heinemann Library
a division of Pearson Inc.
Chicago, Illinois

Customer Service 888-454-2279

Visit our website at www.heinemannlibrary.com

Designed by Richard Parker and Hart McLeod.
Colour Reproduction by Dot Gradations Ltd. UK.
Printed and bound in China by Leo Paper Group

13 12 11 10 09
10 9 8 7 6 5 4 3 2 1

Library of Congress Cataloging-in-Publication Data
Somervill, Barbara A.
  Oral reports / Barbara A. Somervill.
      p. cm. -- (School projects survival guides)
  Includes bibliographical references and index.
   ISBN 978-1-4329-1172-0 (hc) -- ISBN 978-1-4329-1177-5 (pb) 1. Public speaking--Juvenile literature. I. Title.
   PN4129.15.S656 2008
   372.67--dc22
                                2008001148

Acknowledgments
The author and publishers are grateful to the following for permission to reproduce copyright material: The publishers would like to thank the following for permission to reproduce photographs: ©Corbis pp. **4** (Charles Gupton), **12** (Thinkstock), **22** (Ed Bock); ©Getty Images pp. **17** (Minden Pictures/Suzi Eszterhas), **26** (Taxi/Seth Joel); ©Photodisc p. **21**; ©Punchstock (Digital Vision) p. **8**.

Note paper design features with permission of ©istockphoto.com.

Every effort has been made to contact copyright holders of any material reproduced in this book. Any omissions will be rectified in subsequent printings if notice is given to the publisher.

Disclaimer
All Internet addresses (URLs) given in this book were valid at the time of going to press. However, due to the dynamic nature of the Internet, some addresses may have changed or ceased to exist since publication. While the author and the publishers regret any inconvenience this may cause readers, no responsibility for any such changes can be accepted by either the author or the publishers.

Contents

Some words are printed in bold, **like this**. You can find out what they mean by looking in the glossary.

What Is an Oral Report?

Report Planner

Step 1: Write down the assignment and its requirements.

Step 2: Note the due date.

Step 3: Get started right away!

Today's science lesson deals with different **endangered species**. The teacher tells the class how tigers, whales, and gray wolves became endangered in the wild. "Class," she says, "I want each of you to choose an endangered animal to study. In two weeks, you will present an oral report. Tell us how that animal became endangered and what is being done to save the species." Marta takes out her homework planner and writes down the assignment. What animal should she study?

Understand the assignment

Giving an oral report makes many students nervous. However, students give oral reports every day. Answering a question in class is a short oral report. Telling a friend what happened at last night's soccer game is also an oral report.

Understanding the assignment is the first step to a successful oral report. What is the subject of the report? How long does the report need to be? When is it due? Do you need to hand in a written paper or just give an oral report? Should you use a display when giving the report? How will you be graded? If there is any part of the project you do not understand, ask the teacher.

Your teacher can answer any questions that you might have about the oral report.

Types of oral reports

Oral reports, also called speeches or presentations, tell the **audience** something. There are four different jobs that they can do. An oral report can give information. It can **demonstrate** how something works. An oral report can **persuade** the audience. Or it can entertain the audience.

A speech about how an animal species became endangered informs the audience. A science experiment done for the class is a **demonstration**. Television commercials and team coaching persuade the listener. Speakers entertain audiences by telling stories or jokes.

Oral reports may serve several purposes at once. For example, the main purpose of your oral report on an endangered species is to inform the audience. If you begin your report with an **anecdote** about an endangered animal, the report also entertains. If the information is interesting, you might persuade listeners to work toward helping a species survive.

Main Purpose	Type of Oral Report	
To Inform	Biographies Sports Social studies Math principles	History News Directions
To Demonstrate	Math procedures How to build or make something Skills (sports, music, art)	Science experiments Cooking
To Persuade	Debates Arguments Commercials or advertisements	Political speeches Book or movie reviews
To Entertain	Stories Poems Songs or jingles	Jokes Anecdotes

TWIST OF THE TONGUE

Tongue twisters help you develop good speaking skills.
Read this three times quickly:

Sally Shelly sells selfish shellfish.

Parts of the report

An oral report has three main sections: the **introduction**, the **body**, and the **conclusion**. The introduction should grab the listeners' attention. The body provides main ideas and supporting facts. The conclusion wraps up the speech.

An introduction needs to be short and catchy. In some ways, the introduction teases the audience. It grabs the listeners' attention and makes them want to hear more. Experienced speakers often use a fascinating fact, a quote, or a story as a way to introduce their topic.

HELPFUL HINT!

With a speech, listeners cannot go back and reread important material. If something is very important, repeat the information later in your speech.

The body makes up the bulk of the report. In a three-minute speech, the body should take about 2 minutes while the introduction and conclusion take about 30 seconds each. This is where you present your ideas about the topic. It also contains all the facts, details, dates, and other information that supports the main ideas. The body needs to be organized in a clear way.

In the body, introduce a main idea and provide the material that supports it. Repeat key facts to help listeners understand important ideas. For example, you might tell the audience that whales became endangered because of over hunting. Give facts and figures about whale hunting. Then, remind the listeners that hunting threatens the survival of whales.

The conclusion, like the introduction, is short. Leave the audience with something to think about. Wrap up the topic. Make a statement. Ask the audience to take action. Whatever you decide to use for your conclusion, do it quickly.

Make a schedule

To make sure you get your work done on time, begin by setting up a schedule that includes all of the different parts of your project. Start your project early enough to allow plenty of time to get everything finished.

Make a schedule that allows you to get the work done on time. Here is an example:

Monday	Tuesday	Wednesday	Thursday	Friday
Week 1 Choose topic Begin research	Research	Research	Research	Sort information

Monday	Tuesday	Wednesday	Thursday	Friday
Week 2 Write speech	Make note cards. Make display poster	Practice	Practice	Give the report

CHAPTER CHECKLIST
- ✓ I know what is required.
- ✓ I start work immediately.
- ✓ I plan my work in advance.

Choosing a Topic

Marta does not know which endangered animal to study. She reviews a list of endangered species posted on the bulletin board, then she **brainstorms** a list of animals that interest her. She does some **pre-research** in the school library. After seeing what research material is available, Marta picks mountain gorillas for her topic.

Choosing the right topic

Sometimes a teacher assigns specific topics for a report. Other times, students can pick their own topics. If you have a choice, pick a subject that appeals to you. You will have more fun and do a better job if you are interested in the topic.

Be sure to consider your audience when picking a topic. For your oral report to be a success, you must keep the audience's attention. You might be interested in endangered armored snails, but will your audience want to hear about them? You want to choose a topic that will excite the audience.

Do some pre-research to find out if there is enough available material on your topic. Look up the subject on an Internet **search engine** or in the library's **card catalog**. If there is plenty of material available, your **research** will be easier.

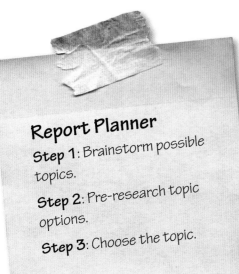

Report Planner

Step 1: Brainstorm possible topics.

Step 2: Pre-research topic options.

Step 3: Choose the topic.

After brainstorming several possible topics, Marta decides to study mountain gorillas.

Expanding or narrowing a topic

A topic can be too large or too small to make a good report subject, so be sure your topic is neither too broad nor too narrow. It would be impossible to talk about all endangered species in a three-minute report. It might also be hard to come up with enough to say about endangered snails or pupfish.

There are many ways to expand or narrow a topic. Begin with the general topic. Think about the topic from different angles. For example, the topic is endangered species. One approach might be to research a specific species. Another idea might be to look at a family of animals. Broaden the topic from a Karner's blue butterfly (too narrow) to endangered North American butterflies (just right).

Try another approach. There are several species of endangered big cats. One way to examine the topic would be to study only tigers. Another idea might be to study all big cats suffering from **habitat** loss. A third idea might be endangered cats of Asia, such as tigers, Asian lions, snow leopards, and so on. Work on your topic until you have enough material to fill your report, but not too much material to cover within the time limit.

Narrow your topic to a reasonable size.

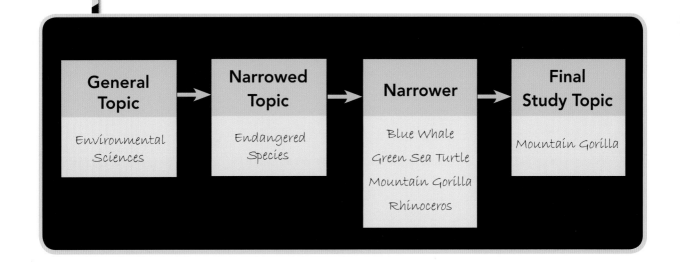

General Topic	Narrowed Topic	Narrower	Final Study Topic
Environmental Sciences	Endangered Species	Blue Whale Green Sea Turtle Mountain Gorilla Rhinoceros	Mountain Gorilla

CHAPTER CHECKLIST

- ✓ I chose a topic.
- ✓ I viewed the topic from different angles.
- ✓ I adjusted the topic to a manageable size.

Doing Research

Marta uses a KWL **graphic organizer** to begin her research on mountain gorillas. KWL stands for "what you Know, what you Want to know, and what you have Learned." Marta writes down what she already knows and what she wants to know. She will fill in the "Learned" box as she does her research.

Finding information

When you research a topic, begin with what you already know. Use that information to guide your research. For example, suppose your topic is tigers. You might want to look for information about tigers, endangered animals, Asian animals, and big cats.

You should look for information in several different books, magazines, or videos. These are called sources. Collect at least three to five sources to find the material you need. You will find information at both school and public libraries and on the Internet.

Report Planner

Step 1: Take a trip to the library.

Step 2: Surf the Internet.

Step 3: Ask an expert for information.

Use a KWL graphic organizer to begin your research.

What you KNOW	What you WANT to know	What you have LEARNED
Mountain gorillas: Endangered Live in Africa	Why endangered? What happened? Who is helping? What stands in the way of survival?	?

Using the library

Libraries are organized to make finding information easy. They have separate sections for fiction and nonfiction books, videos, audiobooks, magazines, newspapers, and **reference** materials.

Begin your research by searching in the card catalog. You can search by title, author, or subject. The catalog lists books, videos, DVDs, and audiotapes. The nonfiction section is organized by the **Dewey decimal system**. Every nonfiction subject has an assigned number. For instance, go to the nonfiction book area, look for 599.758, and you will find books on tigers.

Use a book's table of contents and index to pinpoint the information you are looking for. For example, the table of contents will tell you if there is a chapter specifically on tiger **conservation**. The index will list specific pages where you will find information on habitat loss or over hunting.

HELPFUL HINT!

When you begin looking for research, ask a librarian to help you. Librarians know how to find the best materials for your project.

You should also look for magazine articles on your research topic. Ask the librarian to help you. You may need to access a **subscription database** through the library computer. Use this in the same way you use a search engine. Enter the topic you want researched, and the database will list articles on that topic.

You may be allowed to print out material you find on the Internet. Be sure to ask the librarian if printing is allowed and how many pages you may print. If you cannot print information from the Internet, write the important facts and the source on note cards.

Using the Internet

Many people do research on the Internet, and there is plenty of **reference** material available. The best way to find what you need is to use a search engine. A search engine finds articles and websites on a specific topic in a matter of seconds.

Control your search by defining the narrowest possible topic. Look for "blue whale conservation" rather than just "whales" or "conservation." Enter the subject in the search window, click the "go" button, and poof! You have instant research. You may get thousands of hits—sources and sites—on your topic.

There are several reference websites on the Internet with links to dictionaries, encyclopedias, newspapers, and magazines. Enter "Reference Desk" in your search engine to find such a site, and to ensure that the sites given contain credible information.

Many websites will also have lists of favorite links to other websites on similar topics. Keep a note pad by the computer. Carefully write down the names or addresses of the best sites you find. That way, you can return to those sites again. If you are using your own computer, you might want to bookmark a helpful site.

You may do research at home, at school, or in the library.

If you are studying a current topic, try to use books and articles published in the last five years. Those materials will have the most recent information.

Choosing appropriate information

Once the search list pops up, you must sort trusted sources from those that contain false or inaccurate information. On the Internet, look for sources that have .gov, .org, or .edu in their addresses. Government agencies run .gov websites. Org refers to organizations, such as zoos, museums, charities, or conservation groups. Edu is the address for schools, colleges, and universities. Websites and articles with these addresses usually provide more accurate information than .com sites.

Personal interviews

Experts can be excellent resources. When you ask an expert questions, the process is called an interview. How do you find an expert to interview? Suppose you are researching manatees. There are several organizations that are working to save manatees. These groups have websites on the Internet and contact information. Send an e-mail with your questions to the organization, and you will get a response. You might also find an expert listed in an article about your subject.

Whether you do your interview in person, by phone, or by e-mail, be prepared. Write down five questions you need answered. Be sure to say "thank you" when the interview is over.

CHAPTER CHECKLIST

✓ I used several sources.
✓ I used an Internet search engine.
✓ I used reliable resources.

Organizing Information

Report Planner

Step 1: Sort notes by subjects.

Step 2: Use a graphic organizer.

Step 3: Organize notes in a logical order.

Marta needs to get organized. She collects her notes and decides to arrange her speech according to causes and effects. She has discovered three major reasons why mountain gorillas have become endangered. Marta has also found four fascinating facts about gorillas that she will use in her speech.

Sorting and organizing information

As you do your research, take notes on index cards. These cards come in 3x5, 4x6, or 5x8 sizes. On the top of each card, write the subject, the source, and the page number where the information was found. This will help for sorting notes later on.

Each note should be short. Just write the facts, details, dates, or other important information on the topic in your own words. If you use someone else's words, you must give that person credit for what they said. Using another author's material without giving them credit is called **plagiarism**, and it is against the law.

Every time you change the topic, use a new note card. For example, you research giant pandas. On one note card, you write about what pandas eat. You write about the loss of panda habitats on a different card.

TWIST OF THE TONGUE

Try this tongue twister:

A quick-witted cricket critic.

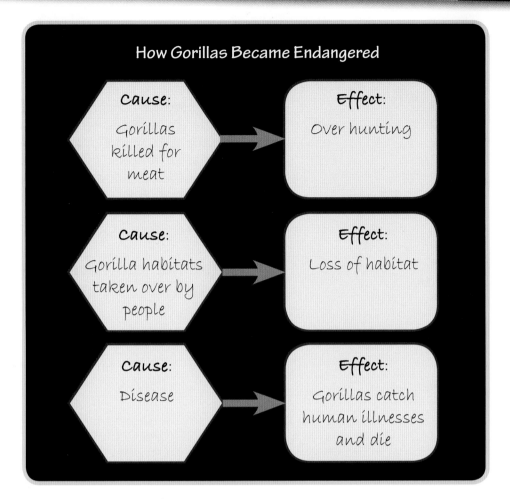

How Gorillas Became Endangered

Cause:
Gorillas killed for meat

→

Effect:
Over hunting

Cause:
Gorilla habitats taken over by people

→

Effect:
Loss of habitat

Cause:
Disease

→

Effect:
Gorillas catch human illnesses and die

Using graphic organizers

Graphic organizers help sort information. Different organizers work well for different types of information. You do not need to use complete sentences in a graphic organizer. Just put the main ideas and facts down in short phrases.

You can find examples of useful graphic organizers at the end of this book or on the Internet. Use an organizer to refine your ideas into smaller categories. Then, sort your note cards according to those categories. Put the note cards in the order in which you plan to use them and number each card. You are almost ready to write your speech.

CHAPTER CHECKLIST

- ✓ I took notes on note cards.
- ✓ I organized subject categories.
- ✓ I put my notes in useful order.

Knowing the Audience

Report Planner

Step 1: Consider what your audience knows.

Step 2: Look for fascinating facts.

Step 3: Use repetition and concrete examples.

Marta needs to consider what her class already knows about her topic. She is sure the class knows that mountain gorillas live in Africa, but the class will not know about the countries of Uganda and Rwanda. She will add some key information about this environment to her speech.

What the audience knows

The **content** of a speech depends on the audience. For example, an oral report given to a class in school would present simpler material than a speech given to scientists. The less the audience already knows, the more you have to explain.

Your audience is made up of classmates. You mostly share the same basic knowledge. As you plan your oral report, ask yourself some questions: What does my audience want to know? What fascinating facts might keep them interested in my report?

Using fascinating facts

Whenever you do research, you will discover some really interesting facts. Become a fascinating fact collector. Sprinkle these facts throughout your report, and you will find your classmates listening to what you say. These facts should fit in with the information given in your report.

What makes a fact fascinating? A common fact is something most people already know. A fascinating fact is something outrageous, unbelievable, weird, or interesting. A common fact is that blue whales have tongues. A fascinating fact is that their tongues are so big that a full-sized elephant could stand on one and have room left over!

For the first three months of a baby gorilla's life, its mother never puts it down—not even when she sleeps. This is an example of a fascinating fact.

HELPFUL HINT!

Look up fascinating facts about your topic. If you can quickly find five or more interesting facts, you have the start for an exciting oral report.

Helping your listener

Listeners will understand your report better if you provide some help. **Repetition** is a key "helper." Repeat important facts, figures, or ideas. Change the wording when you repeat the material, but be sure to repeat main ideas and supporting facts.

The information you give should be **concrete**. In a speech, concrete information includes solid, actual facts that make a point. It is one thing to say, "Whaling killed lots of whales." It is better to say, "During the 1900s, about 360,000 blue whales were killed by hunters in the Antarctic alone."

CHAPTER CHECKLIST

✓ I considered my audience.
✓ I found fascinating facts.
✓ I plan to use repetition and concrete facts.

Writing and Revising

Report Planner

Step 1: Plan a short opening statement.

Step 2: Use an outline or graphic organizer for the body.

Step 3: Wrap up quickly at the end.

Marta is not sure how to write an oral report, so she asks her teacher what to do. The teacher suggests that Marta write only the introduction and the conclusion. She tells Marta to use an outline or main idea organizer for the body of the report. She says, "Speak from your notes instead of reading your report word for word."

Writing the report

An oral report needs to grab the audience from the first sentence. The introduction is short—three or four sentences make a good opener. Use the introduction to catch the listeners' attention and announce the topic.

There are several standard types of introductions that interest an audience. Some speakers start with a quote. The quote chosen should come from an expert or a well-known person. Another good opener is a fascinating fact. Tell the fact, and then draw the audience in by explaining how that fact connects to your topic. Another idea might be to connect your report to others heard before. Begin with "You know what has happened to tigers and manatees. Now, I'm going to tell you what is happening with rhinos, and the news is not good."

HELPFUL HINT! Use a highlighter to highlight key words, phrases, facts, or quotes in your report. This will help you find your place as you speak.

The body—outline or organizer

Now you are ready to work on the body of your speech. This is the longest part—about two-thirds of the report. Unless your teacher asks you to hand in a written version of your report, the body does not need to be written out word for word. What you really need is a guide to organize your main ideas and supporting facts.

An outline is one way to arrange material in the order in which it is to be presented. Outlines have three basic parts: main ideas, subtopics, and supporting details. Follow the sample graphic below for the general layout of an outline.

A main idea organizer is another way to arrange information. Use one page or large note card for each main idea. Write the idea in a box on the left of the page or note card. List two or three supporting facts or details on the right-hand side. See a sample of a main idea organizer on page 29 of this book.

Make an outline to organize your material. Here is an example:

Mountain Gorillas

I. Habitat
   A. Rwanda
   B. Uganda
   C. Mountain Forests

II. Reasons They Are Endangered
   A. Poaching or Hunting
   B. Loss of Habitat
   C. Disease

III. Helping Gorillas
   A. Organizations
      1. International Gorilla Conservation Program
      2. Conservation and Research for Endangered Species
      3. Mountain Gorilla Conservation Fund
   B. Dian Fossey
   C. Zoos

Writing the conclusion

A conclusion needs to be as short as the introduction. Three or four sentences are enough. Begin by restating the main idea of your report. Then, end the same way you began. Use a quote, a fascinating fact, or some connection to other information in your report. You might also use a call to action. Ask people to do something. For example, "We can help whooping cranes survive. Let's adopt a whooper through the national zoo!"

Making note cards

You can give your oral report from full-sized pages, but index cards are easier to manage. Transfer your notes onto index cards. Try not to put too many words on any card. You want the notes to remind you of what to say, not record every word. Just record the important facts or phrases that will serve as **cues** as you speak.

When you use quotes, write each quote on a note card. Mark the place where the quote belongs in your outline or organizer. You should give the author credit for what is said. Say something such as, "According to Jane Goodall, an expert on chimpanzees…" Do not try to memorize the quote—just read it.

Be sure to number each card in order of use. If your cards get out of order, you can quickly sort them. When you have your notes in order, do your first practice speech.

Here is a sample note card:

Chimpanzees	Jane Goodall, 2006 Interview, *Sierra Magazine*	Card #5
	"Worldwide there are more human children born every day than the total number of great apes left in the wild, which is about 300,000 at the most and decreasing all the time."	

Revising the report

Time your speech by using a clock. Do not stop for mistakes or to reword a section. How long did the report take? Did it meet the assignment's requirements? If your report runs short, you need to add more information. If it is too long, think about what can be removed without harming the report.

When speaking in front of a group, you will talk faster than during practice. A practice speech that takes four minutes will probably last less than three minutes in front of an audience. Keep this in mind to ensure your speech will meet the minimum time requirement.

When practicing your oral report, use a clock to check that the report is within the time limits your teacher assigned.

CHAPTER CHECKLIST

✓ I wrote a catchy opener.
✓ I arranged notes for the body.
✓ I made note cards.

Visual Aids

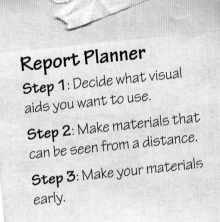

Marta's oral report is ready, but she feels the report needs some visual help. She thinks a map of eastern Africa with locations of mountain gorilla populations might help. She would also like to show pictures of mountain gorillas in their natural habitat.

Posters

Posters are usually viewed from a distance. The pictures and words need to be large. This can be hard to do. When you work on a poster, everything is close and looks the correct size. Your audience will not be so close. Test the **visibility** of your poster from at least 15 feet (4.5 meters) away.

Posters are a good way to show charts and graphs, pictures, diagrams of how something works, and illustrations. Be sure to provide a headline on your poster and readable labels of key items.

If your classroom already has a map, you might use that one instead of making your own map.

Maps

Maps are ideal for showing your audience where something took place or where something is located. Use maps in history, social studies, or science reports when the place is important. Include the area and enough surrounding land to help the audience relate to the place discussed. For instance, Galapagos tortoises are only found on the Galapagos Islands, but where are they? A map of the islands is good; a map that shows the islands' distance from a known place, such as South America, is better.

Handouts

Sometimes an idea is too difficult or needs too much explanation for a poster. If so, you might think about making a handout. Handouts are good for complicated diagrams or illustrations, extensive scientific procedures, or history timelines.

Demonstrations and experiments

There is nothing that makes a science report as exciting as doing a demonstration in class. Demonstrations and experiments are a good way to show an audience how to make something or how a process works. Such displays work well for science, math, cooking, and woodworking. Explain your idea completely to your teacher and ask permission to do your demonstration or experiment. You would also need to test your experiment to make sure it works, and bring all materials with you.

Models

A model is a three-dimensional display of a process, a structure of some type, a scene, or a moment in history. A **diorama** of a scene from a book or a play adds to an oral book report. Models of an explorer's ship would interest an audience, as would a model of an early telephone or a miniature bridge or castle.

CHAPTER CHECKLIST

✓ I chose useful visual aids.
✓ I made the materials early.
✓ I tested the materials from a distance.

Practice, Practice, Practice

Report Planner

Step 1: Practice your report several times alone.

Step 2: Ask family or friends to be an audience.

Step 3: Use visual aids when practicing.

Marta needs an audience. Her older brother has done dozens of oral reports in school, so she asks him to listen to her. She sets up her poster and map in front of the living room sofa and begins. "Mountain gorillas are nearly human. They have families, love their children, and share meals together. Sadly, their greatest threat to survival comes from one of their closest relatives—humans."

Personal practice

A good speech must be practiced several times. Set up your presentation in front of a mirror and then talk to yourself. Present the report from beginning to end, including drawing attention to your visual aids.

On a separate note card write something like: TALK ABOUT MAP HERE. Highlight this so that you do not read it by mistake. Insert the note card in the exact place where you wish to discuss the visual aid. This will remind you to call attention to a poster, map, or graph at the right time.

Go through your complete speech, and then make notes on areas that need work. Go over the rough areas at least twice. Then, repeat the entire speech from the beginning. Keep practicing until you have a smooth, easy presentation, but don't try to memorize it.

Using your voice and body

If you are nervous talking in front of a group, you need to work on your voice. Make sure you speak loudly enough to be heard from the back of the room. Practice talking slowly and clearly.

Before you begin speaking, think about your voice and your body. Stand up straight and smile. Take just a moment to collect your thoughts, breathe deeply, and begin.

A sample audience

Two days before you are due to deliver your report, practice in front of an audience. This practice will be a **dress rehearsal**. Ask your audience—your parents, friends, or other family members—to time your report for you. Once you begin, go through to the end even if you make mistakes. When you are done, ask for helpful suggestions to improve your report. Work on the areas that need improvement and ask your audience to listen again the next day.

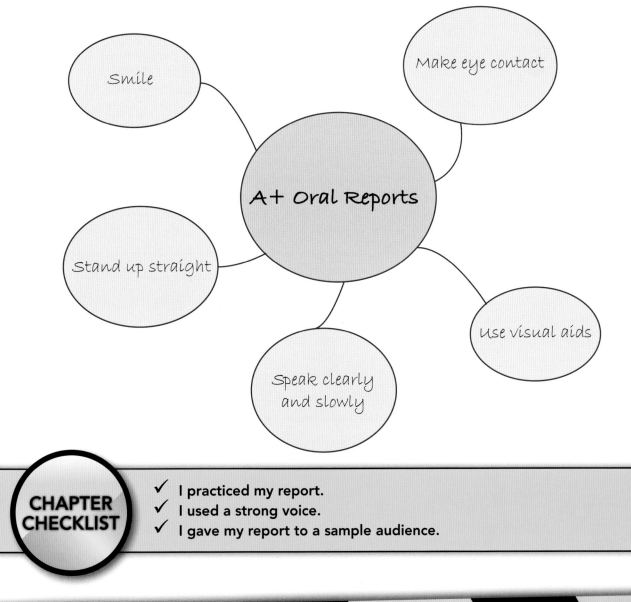

CHAPTER CHECKLIST

✓ I practiced my report.
✓ I used a strong voice.
✓ I gave my report to a sample audience.

Presenting the Report

Report Planner

Step 1: Handle stage fright.

Step 2: Use good presentation skills.

Step 3: Smile!

Marta brings her note cards and visual aids to school. Just before she is to give her report, Marta breathes slowly several times to calm her nerves. She reviews her note cards before getting up in front of the class. She is confident that she will do well. The teacher says, "Marta, are you ready?" Marta smiles.

Stage fright

The jitters you feel just before you give a speech are natural. You have stage fright. Even the most experienced actors and politicians feel butterflies in their stomachs before a big event. The best cure for stage fright is knowing your material. If you've done the work and practiced, your oral report will go fine.

Before you begin speaking try these three relaxation techniques: Take a few deep breaths. Then, clench your hands tightly and relax them three times. Finally, imagine yourself going through your speech calmly. See yourself as a success.

See yourself as a success—and you will be!

HELPFUL HINT!

If you make a mistake, smile, collect your thoughts, and keep going. Don't let one tiny error take over your oral report.

Look around the audience and pick a friendly face. When you begin speaking, pretend you are only talking to that friend. As you relax, you can look around the room and make eye contact with others. Concentrate on what you are saying so that you won't be distracted.

Presentation skills

Giving a speech from note cards may seem difficult, but it is really the easiest method. Reading a report can become boring to the audience. Memorizing takes too much time, and you may forget something and get confused. Note cards produce the best result for you and your audience.

Be sure to speak clearly, slowly, and with **expression**. Breathe evenly, pausing when appropriate. Stand up straight and, above all, smile. Relax, you do not have to be perfect.

What did you learn?

Throughout your life, you will be called on to speak in front of many groups. You may become a teacher, a lawyer, or a doctor. You may be a sports announcer, a news reporter, or a radio chat host. You will work with other people, and you will need to explain your ideas and actions. Oral reports are part of everyday life. So, take a deep breath, smile… and begin.

CHAPTER CHECKLIST

✓ I have my materials ready.
✓ I practiced.
✓ I will be successful!

Graphic Organizers

Graphic organizers help you sort research, understand materials, and study for tests. Choose one that fits your needs.

Cycle of Events

Use a cycle of events organizer to record a continuing process, such as the life cycle of a butterfly or the water cycle.

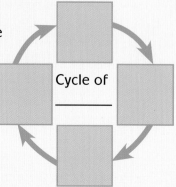

Chain of Events

When trying to organize a sequence of events, use a chain of events organizer. It is particularly good for arranging information for demonstrations or for a biography or history project.

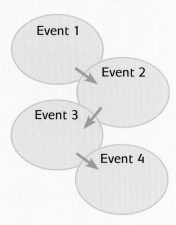

Cause and Effect

A cause-and-effect chart allows you to relate events (causes) and the results (effects) of those events. A cause-and-effect chart works well for discussing scientific processes, historic events, and how or why something happened.

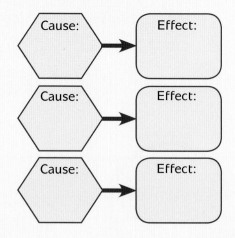

Idea Web

An idea web helps you focus on the main idea and supporting information.

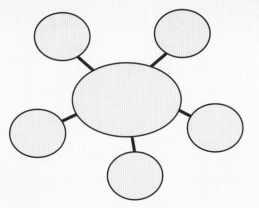

KWL (Know-Want-Learn)

Complete the "K" section of the KWL organizer by providing information you already know about the topic. Determine what you want to learn and note it under "W." As you do your research, add new information under the "L" section.

What you KNOW	What you WANT to know	What you have LEARNED

Main Idea

Use this organizer to identify the main idea of a passage or paragraph and the information that supports the main idea.

	Supporting Information:
Main Idea:	Supporting Information:
	Supporting Information:

Research Resources

In the Library

Almanacs
An almanac is published every year. It contains facts, figures, and statistics on many different topics. Be sure to use the most recent edition to get current facts.

Atlases
An atlas is a book of maps, usually covering the entire world. Additional maps may show the oceans, ocean currents, topography, how land is used, agriculture, and population.

Dictionaries
Most dictionaries do more than just tell definitions of words. Standard dictionaries may contain synonyms, antonyms, usage, word origin, and pronunciation. There are also biographical and geographical dictionaries.

Encyclopedias
An encyclopedia contains information on a wide variety of subjects. There are also narrower versions, such as an encyclopedia of mammals, sports, plants, and so on.

Reader's Guide to Periodical Literature
This guide is an index for magazines, newspapers, and journals. It covers 400 sources and goes back as far as 1983.

School or Public Librarians
The first stop you should make when doing research is a visit to a librarian. Librarians know how to find information and how to get that information for you.

On the Internet

Homework Help
There are many sites that offer help with homework. HomeworkSpot.com also offers suggestions on science projects, staying healthy, and arts and crafts, among other topics.

Internet Public Library
The Internet Public Library (www.ipl.org) is like having a library on your desktop computer. You can search through the site for information on social studies, science, medicine, literature, and so on. You can read a book, a magazine, or a newspaper.

Online News
Most major newspapers, news magazines, and television stations have news websites. Many have search windows. Enter your topic and click "search."

Search Engines
Search engines have many interesting names—Ask.com, Google, and Yahoo, to name a few. Each of these search engines works in the same way. Enter a topic in the search window, click, and the engine finds articles and websites that fill your request. Be patient. You may not find what you need on the first attempt.

Glossary

anecdote short, personal story of an incident or event

audience group of people who watch and listen to a presentation

body main section of a speech or written piece

brainstorm come up with quick ideas on a topic

card catalog tool for finding library materials by author, title, or subject

conclusion end of a speech or written piece

concrete certain and specific, rather than vague or general

conservation act of saving or preserving something, such as an animal or plant species

content material or ideas in a document, book, or other source

cue something said, done, or written that reminds someone to do or say something

demonstrate show how something works

demonstration display given to others to show how something is done or how something works

Dewey decimal system system of arranging nonfiction materials by assigning numbers to specific topics

diorama three-dimensional representation of a scene, such as those seen in museums

dress rehearsal practice of something that will be presented to an audience

endangered on the verge of extinction or no longer being in existence

expression way of communicating thoughts, feelings, or information

graphic organizer visual aid for sorting information

habitat natural conditions in which a plant or animal lives

introduction opening of a speech or written piece

persuade convince someone

plagiarism use someone else's written ideas without giving them credit for the material

pre-research look into a topic before beginning the actual project

reference source of information

repetition process of saying or writing something again

research look up information about a subject

search engine program on the Internet designed to find articles and websites on specific topics

species basic biological classification of an animal or plant

subscription database collection of magazine articles, quotes, documents, or pictures

visibility being able to be clearly seen

Index